INDIAN COOKING

Cooking Utensils

Most Western kitchens are well equipped for the preparation of Indian food. Currying is basically a stewing process, so a large heavy saucepan is all that is needed. When deep-frying – semosas or koftas – for example, use normal deep-frying equipment. Chapattis are traditionally cooked on a dome-shaped disc called a *tawa*, but a frying pan or any flat metal plate is perfectly adequate.

INDIAN COOKING

Edited by
Eileen Turner

CONTENTS

**First published in hardcover in 1978 by
Octopus Books Limited
59 Grosvenor Street, London W1**

This edition published in 1983

© 1978 Octopus Books Limited

ISBN 0 7064 2016 0

Produced by Mandarin Publishers Limited
22a Westland Road
Quarry Bay, Hong Kong

Printed in Hong Kong

Frontispiece: CIDER FISH CURRY WITH ACCOMPANIMENTS *(page 14)*
(Photograph: Taunton Cider)

Weights and Measures

All measurements in this book are based on Imperial weights and measures, with American equivalents given in parenthesis.

Measurements in *weight* in the Imperial and American system are the same. Measurements in *volume* are different, and the following table shows the equivalents:

Spoon measurements

Imperial	U.S.
1 tablespoon	1 tablespoon
1½ tablespoons	2 tablespoons
2 tablespoons	3 tablespoons (abbrev: T)

Level spoon measurements are used in all the recipes.

Liquid measurements

1 Imperial pint	20 fluid ounces
1 American pint	16 fluid ounces
1 American cup	8 fluid ounces

INTRODUCTION

The basic art of Indian cooking lies in the careful blending of different spices to yield subtle variations in flavours. Curries form the mainstay of the Indian cuisine. A curry is basically a casserole of fish, shellfish, poultry, meat or vegetables cooked in a sauce, the flavour of which is created by the combination of the flavours of the spices added during cooking.

The origin of curries can be traced back many centuries. When there was no means of keeping perishable food fresh, meat, fish and poultry rapidly acquired an unpleasant taint in the hot, humid Indian climate. Spices were therefore added to disguise the distasteful flavour of the main ingredient. Generally the hotter the local climate, the greater the problem of food preservation and the hotter the curry!

Regional differences in religion, culture and local produce have also influenced eating habits to yield an intriguing diversity of exotic, tasty dishes. The hottest curries come from Southern India. Most of the inhabitants of this part of the country are Hindus, who never eat beef but sometimes eat other meat and fish. Vegetable dishes often form the main course of their meals and many of the spicy vegetable curries and recipes for stuffed aubergines and samosas originate from this region.

Traditionally the cooler north is associated with milder curries. The Muslim community is found mainly in the north and also around Bombay. Muslims will generally eat beef and lamb but never pork. Meat dishes such as keema pimento, kofta curry, seekh kababs and roghan gosht originally came from Northern India.

When serving an Indian meal, aim to select a variety of dishes which complement each other in texture and flavour. Samosas or prawn puffs may be served as appetizers. Main-course dishes should be served with a selection of sambals or side dishes. For entertaining, choose several main-course dishes based on a variety of main ingredients and with different amounts and combinations of spices. Freshly cooked chappatis, puris and pappadoms are delicious accompaniments. Complete the meal with a refreshing dessert, such as gulab jamon or jelabis.

8   BEEF CURRY WITH ACCOMPANIMENTS *(page 56)*
(Photograph: The Rice Council)

Guide to Ingredients

Curry powder: There are many varieties of curry powder on the market, but they are all a mixture of various spices used in Indian cooking. Where curry powder is called for in a recipe, use a commercial one or mix your own. You may like to try the following recipe, then experiment with different spices to evolve your own curry powder.

2 tablespoons (3T) coriander seeds

2 tablespoons (3T) cumin seeds

5 chillies

5 cardamoms

1 tablespoon garam masala

1 teaspoon fenugreek

1 teaspoon ground ginger

2 tablespoons (3T) ground turmeric

Using an electric grinder or a pestle and mortar, grind together all the spices except the turmeric. Then mix in the turmeric and sieve the mixture if necessary. Store in an air-tight jar for up to 1 month.

Chillis: The seeds of a chilli pepper are very hot so if you wish to reduce the strength of the curry remove the seeds before adding the chilli.

Coconut milk: Put ½ lb. (2⅔ cups) desiccated (shredded) coconut in a bowl and pour on 1 pint (2½ cups) boiling water. Place in an electric blender and emulsify for 30 seconds or leave to soak for 20 minutes. Then pour through a fine strainer, squeezing the pulp to extract all the liquid. Discard the coconut pulp and add a pinch of salt to the liquid.

Effect of different spices: Knowing what effect each spice will have on a dish comes mainly with experience, but the following guide may be useful.

For hotness add chilli powder or whole chillies.

For sweetness add coriander or garam masala.

For sourness add cumin, fenugreek or cardamoms.

Sugar can be used to increase the sweetness of a dish, and milk or yogurt can be used to reduce hotness and thicken the sauce.

Frying ground spices: Spices should be fried at a high temperature to bring out their flavour. If, after a minute or two, the spice mixture becomes dry and brown add a few drops of water.

Ghee: This is a form of clarified butter and is used for frying. It is available in most Indian shops but if you cannot get it, use oil or butter instead.

Alternatively, prepare clarified butter. Melt 1 lb. (2 cups) butter in a heavy pan over gentle heat and cook, without stirring, until the butter begins to foam. Skim off the foam and continue heating without browning, skimming frequently, until the butter stops foaming.

Let the butter cool until the sediment has sunk to the bottom of the pan. Pour the liquid through muslin or cheesecloth into a container, making sure none of the sediment is poured off.

Cover and leave the butter to set. Store in a refrigerator until required.

SNACKS AND COCKTAIL SAVOURIES

Alu Ke Lachche Savoury Potato Straws

2 medium potatoes
oil for deep frying
½ teaspoon salt

¾ teaspoon ground caraway
  seeds
pinch of cayenne pepper

Peel, wash and shred the potatoes. Drain and spread them out on a wooden board to dry. Heat the oil and deep fry the potatoes until golden brown. Drain on kitchen paper. Combine the salt and spices and mix with the potatoes. Serve hot or cold.
Makes about ¾ lb. (2 cups)

Prawn (Shrimp) Puffs

½ lb. (1⅓ cups) cooked shelled
  prawns (shrimp)
1 onion, chopped
2 oz. (¼ cup) ghee or butter
1 teaspoon ground coriander
1 teaspoon ground turmeric
½ teaspoon ground cumin

3 tablespoons (¼ cup) cold water
3 tablespoons (¼ cup) boiling
  water
salt
12 oz. packet frozen puff pastry
  (puff paste)
beaten egg or milk to glaze

Clean the prawns, then mince (grind) them into a paste. Fry the onion in the ghee or butter until brown.

Mix the coriander, turmeric and cumin with the cold water to form a paste, then add the same quantity of boiling water. Stir the mixture into the onion and cook, stirring, for 3 minutes. Then add the prawn paste and salt and cook gently for 5 minutes. Leave the mixture to cool.

Roll out the pastry very thinly and cut it into 3 inch squares. Fill the centre of each generously with the prawn mixture. Damp the pastry edges and fold each square corner to corner, to make triangles, sealing well. Brush with beaten egg or milk and place on a baking sheet. Bake in a moderately hot oven, 400°F, Gas Mark 6 for about 25 minutes, until the puffs are golden brown.
Makes about 30 puffs

Samosas Curried Meat Puffs

4 oz. (1 cup) plain (all-purpose)
 flour
salt
1 oz. (2T) butter
2 tablespoons (3T) warm milk
1 onion, finely chopped
¼ teaspoon garlic powder
2 oz. (¼ cup) ghee or oil
1 green chilli, seeded and finely
 chopped

½ lb. (1 cup) lean minced
 (ground) lamb or beef
1 tomato, skinned and chopped
1 tablespoon ground coriander
¼ teaspoon chilli powder
¼ teaspoon garam masala
2 teaspoons lemon juice
oil for deep frying

Sift the flour with a pinch of salt, then rub in the butter until the mixture resembles fine breadcrumbs. Stir in the milk and knead thoroughly until a smooth dough is formed. Cover with a plate and leave for 1 hour.

Fry the onion and garlic powder in the ghee or oil until golden brown. Add the green chilli and fry for 2 minutes. Then add the meat and continue frying, stirring occasionally, until the meat turns brown. Add the tomato, coriander, chilli powder and garam masala with salt to taste. Stir well and simmer gently for 20 minutes or until the meat is tender. Then stir in the lemon juice and leave to cool.

Divide the pastry into 6 portions and roll each one out to form a circle about ⅛ inch thick. Cut each circle in half and place a tablespoonful of the meat filling in the centre of each semi-circle.

Damp the edges of the pastry and fold over to form a triangular shape. Seal the edges well. Heat the oil and deep fry the samosas, a few at a time, until they are golden brown. Drain on kitchen paper and serve hot.
Makes 12

Vegetable samosas:
Use 4 oz. (⅔ cup) diced potato and 4 oz. (¾ cup) shelled peas instead of the meat. Cook the potatoes and peas before adding them to the pan, then simmer for 2 minutes. Simmer for 5 minutes only, after adding the tomato and spices.

Bhune Kaju Cashews

12 oz. (2 cups) cashew nuts
1½ tablespoons (2T) butter
1 teaspoon salt

¼ teaspoon cayenne pepper
½ teaspoon ground cumin

Fry the cashew nuts in the butter over moderate heat until they are golden brown. Drain on kitchen paper. Combine the salt, cayenne pepper and cumin and toss the nuts in this mixture. Serve hot or cold.
Makes about ¾ lb. (2 cups)

CHICKEN CIDER CURRY WITH RICE *(page 34)*
(Photograph: British Poultry Meat Association)

FISH

Cider Fish Curry

½ lb. haddock fillet
½ pint (1¼ cups) milk and water
  mixed
salt
freshly ground black pepper
2 oz. (¼ cup) butter
1 onion, finely chopped
1 oz. (¼ cup) flour
1 level tablespoon curry powder
¾ pint (2 cups) dry (hard) cider

1 oz. (3T) sultanas (seedless white
  raisins)
1 oz. (¼ cup) walnuts, chopped
1 dessert apple, cored and sliced
3 oz. (½ cup) cooked shelled
  prawns (shrimp)
8 oz. (1⅓ cups) rice, soaked for 30
  minutes in cold water
1 small bay leaf

Poach the haddock in the milk and water with seasoning to taste and 1 oz. (2T) of the butter until tender. When cooked, drain the fish and remove the skin and any bones. Flake the fish carefully.

Melt the remaining butter in a pan and gently fry the onion until it is soft but not brown. Mix in the flour and curry powder and cook for 1 minute. Gradually stir in the cider and bring to the boil, stirring until the sauce thickens. Stir in the sultanas, walnuts and apple, then add the flaked fish. Mix in most of the prawns, reserving a few for decoration.

Drain the rice and cook in 1 pint (2½ cups) boiling salted water with the bay leaf until just tender. Drain thoroughly and arrange it in a ring on a warm serving dish. If wished, arrange the rice on an ovenproof dish and place in a warm oven for a few minutes to dry. Pile the curry in the middle of the dish and sprinkle with the remaining prawns.

Serve with pappadoms and a selection of accompaniments. A dish of sliced hard-boiled eggs and bananas goes well with this curry.
Serves 4

Parsee Machi Fish in Parsee Sauce

1 lb. filleted white fish
3 cloves garlic
1 teaspoon ground cumin
½ teaspoon chilli powder
2 tablespoons (3T) oil
2 onions, sliced
3 chillies
¾ pint (2 cups) water

salt
¾ tablespoon cornflour
 (cornstarch)
1 egg
4 tablespoons (⅓ cup) vinegar
sugar
lemon wedges to garnish

Cut the fish into 8 pieces. Crush the garlic and mix it to a paste with the cumin and chilli powder.

Heat the oil in a large pan. Add the onions and sauté until they are golden brown. Then add the whole chillies and the garlic and spice paste. Continue frying for about 1 minute until the spices darken.

Pour in the water and simmer for 5 minutes. Add salt to taste. Mix the cornflour to a smooth paste with a little cold water, then stir it into the sauce.

Add the fish pieces to the sauce and simmer until the fish is tender, stirring gently. Beat the egg with the vinegar and stir it into the sauce. Add sugar to taste and simmer for 2-3 minutes. Transfer to a warmed serving dish. Garnish with lemon wedges and serve with fried rice.
Serves 4

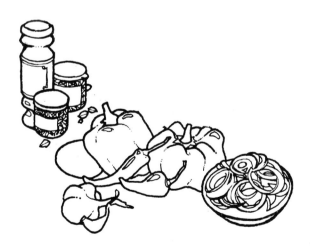

Curried Cod with Peppers

2 lb. cod fillet, cut into 4 serving
  pieces
2 tablespoons (3T) lemon juice
1 tablespoon olive oil
1 teaspoon mustard
salt and pepper
Sauce:
2 oz. (¼ cup) butter
1 large onion, chopped
1 clove garlic, finely chopped

2 tablespoons (3T) flour
1 tablespoon curry powder
¼ teaspoon ground cinnamon
¼ teaspoon ground ginger
1 tablespoon tomato purée (paste)
1 tablespoon lemon juice
¾ pint (2 cups) fish or chicken
  stock (bouillon)
3 small green peppers, cored,
  seeded and sliced into rings

Skin the cod portions and place in a shallow ovenproof dish. Mix together
the lemon juice, olive oil, mustard and a little salt and pepper. Pour the
mixture over the fish and leave to marinate for 3-4 hours.

To make the sauce, melt the butter in a pan over moderate heat. Add
the onion and fry gently until it is soft but not brown. Then stir in the garlic,
flour, curry powder, cinnamon and ginger. Cook over low heat for 3
minutes, stirring all the time. Then add the tomato purée and lemon juice
and stir in the stock. Bring to the boil and simmer until the sauce thickens,
stirring all the time. Taste and add salt and pepper.

Cover the pan with a lid and simmer gently for 30 minutes, stirring
occasionally. Ten minutes before the sauce is ready, add the sliced green
peppers.

Meanwhile, drain the fish. Cover and bake in a moderately hot oven
375°F, Gas Mark 5 for 15-25 minutes, depending on the thickness of the
fillets.

Place the fish fillets on a warm serving dish. Add any juices from the fish
to the curry sauce, then pour over the fillets. Serve with pappadoms and a
crisp green salad.

Serves 4

CURRIED COD WITH PEPPERS AND ACCOMPANIMENTS
(Photograph: White Fish Kitchen)

Machi Pulao Fish Pulao

1 lb. (2⅔ cups) long-grain rice
1 ½ lb. filleted white fish
1 tablespoon ground coriander
2 teaspoons ground cumin
½ teaspoon ground turmeric
½ teaspoon fenugreek
pinch of ground ginger

4 tablespoons (⅓ cup) oil
salt
2 large onions, finely chopped
2 tablespoons (3T) desiccated
 (shredded) coconut
juice of ½ lemon

Wash the rice and leave it to soak in cold water for at least 1 hour. Cut the fish into 2 inch pieces.

Mix the coriander, cumin, turmeric, fenugreek and ginger together. Heat 2 tablespoons (3T) of the oil in a large frying pan (skillet) and fry the spice mixture for about 1 minute. Then place the fish in the pan. Pour in just enough water to cover the fish and add salt to taste. Simmer until the fish is cooked, then remove it carefully with a fish slice and keep warm. Reserve the liquid.

Meanwhile, fry the onions in the remaining oil until brown. Drain the rice and add it to the onions. Mix well, then add the reserved fish liquid, the coconut and lemon juice. Simmer gently until the rice is cooked, adding extra water during cooking when necessary but make sure that when the rice is tender the liquid has been absorbed.

Place the rice in a warm serving dish. Arrange the fish pieces on top of the rice before serving.

Serves 4-6

18

Curried Prawn (Shrimp) Salad

1 small cauliflower, divided into
  florets
salt
8 fl. oz. (1 cup) mayonnaise
½ teaspoon garam masala
½ teaspoon paprika
1 green chilli, finely chopped

3 spring onions (scallions), finely
  chopped
1 lb. (2⅔ cups) cooked shelled
  prawns (shrimp)
½ lettuce, washed
few coriander leaves or mint
  leaves, chopped

Cook the cauliflower in boiling salted water for about 5 minutes, so that it is still quite firm. Leave to cool.

Blend the mayonnaise with the garam masala, paprika, chilli pepper and spring onions. Toss the cauliflower and prawns in the flavoured mayonnaise.

Serve on a bed of lettuce and sprinkle the coriander or mint leaves over the top.
Serves 4

Machi Kabab Spiced Fish Patties

1¼ lb. cod or haddock, cooked
1 large onion, finely chopped
2 potatoes, cooked and mashed
2 green chillies, finely chopped
few coriander leaves, finely
  chopped
½ inch piece of fresh root ginger,
  finely chopped

¼ teaspoon chilli powder
salt
freshly ground black pepper
2 eggs, beaten
dry breadcrumbs for coating
shallow oil for frying
lemon wedges to garnish

Remove the bones from the fish and mash the flesh. Mix in the onion and the mashed potatoes. Then stir in the whole chillies, coriander, ginger and chilli powder. Season to taste with salt and pepper. Add 1 beaten egg to bind the mixture.

Divide the mixture into 8 pieces. Roll into balls then flatten them into rounds, about ½ inch thick. Dip the patties in beaten egg, then coat with breadcrumbs. Fry on both sides in shallow oil until brown. Garnish with lemon wedges.
Serves 4

Fish Curry

6 oz. (1 cup) long-grain rice,
  soaked for 30 minutes in cold
  water
6 fillets of sole or plaice (flounder)
½ pint (1 ¼ cups) dry white wine
  or fish stock (bouillon)
2 large onions, chopped
2 tablespoons (3T) oil

1 teaspoon curry powder
2 tomatoes, skinned and chopped
paprika
Sauce:
2 oz. (¼ cup) butter
1 teaspoon curry powder
2 oz. (½ cup) flour
1 egg yolk

Drain the rice and cook in ¾ pint (2 cups) boiling salted water until just tender. Drain and dry it off in a warm oven. Roll up the fillets of fish and gently poach them in the white wine or fish stock until tender.

Meanwhile fry the onions in the oil until soft but not brown. Add the curry powder and tomatoes and cook for a further 5 minutes, stirring occasionally. Arrange the rice round the edge of a serving dish and sprinkle it with paprika. Spoon the curry mixture into the centre of the rice. Drain the fish fillets, reserving the liquor, and arrange them on top of the curry mixture. Fill the centres of the rolled fish fillets with any remaining curry mixture. Keep warm.

To make the sauce, melt the butter and gently fry the curry powder for 2 minutes. Then stir in the flour and cook for a further 1 minute. Add the reserved cooking liquid gradually, stirring constantly, and bring to the boil, stirring until the sauce thickens. Then stir in the egg yolk and cook without boiling for another 1 minute.

Pour a little of the sauce over the fish and serve the rest separately. Serve with lemon wedges and side dishes of choice. A good accompaniment for this curry is a dish of sliced bananas.
Serves 3

Malabaria Jhinga Grilled Prawns (Shrimp)

1 lb. (3 cups) uncooked prawns
  (shrimp)
6 tablespoons (½ cup) water
salt
1 teaspoon ground coriander
½ teaspoon dried (instant minced)
  onion

12 peppercorns
2 oz. (¼ cup) butter
½ teaspoon ground cumin
1 teaspoon ground turmeric
2 teaspoons lemon or lime juice
8 lemon or lime wedges

Peel and devein the prawns (shrimp) and set them aside. Pour the water
into a large pan. Add 1 teaspoon salt, ½ teaspoon of the coriander, the
onion and the peppercorns. Bring to boiling point, then add the prawns
(shrimp) and cook for 2 minutes, or until they begin to turn pink. Remove
the pan from the heat and drain off the water.

Melt the butter in a pan. Add salt, the remaining spices and lemon or
lime juice. Turn the mixture into a shallow flameproof dish or grill (broiler)
pan and spread the prawns (shrimp) over the surface. Grill for 5 minutes.
Serve with the lemon or lime wedges.
Serves 8

Prawn (Shrimp)
and Tomato Curry

1 lb. (3 cups) uncooked prawns
  (shrimp), shelled and deveined
salt
2 oz. (¼ cup) butter or ghee
3 large tomatoes, skinned and
  sliced
3 onions, finely chopped
¼ teaspoon garlic powder

¼ teaspoon ground ginger
1 teaspoon chilli powder
2 teaspoons ground coriander
½ teaspoon ground turmeric
2 tablespoons (3T) desiccated
  (shredded) coconut
¼ pint (⅔ cup) water
2 teaspoons garam masala

Sprinkle the prawns (shrimp) with salt and lightly fry them in butter or
ghee. Add the tomatoes, onions and all the spices except the garam
masala. Continue to cook for 5 minutes.

Add the coconut and the water and simmer until the prawns are almost
cooked. Then sprinkle on the garam masala and cook until the prawns are
tender. Serve with plain boiled rice and a selection of side dishes.
Serves 3-4

Fried Fish Curry

1½ lb. filleted sole or any firm
  white fish
juice of 1 small lime
¼ teaspoon dry mustard
½ teaspoon chilli powder
pinch of salt
flour for coating
oil for shallow frying
1 oz. (2T) butter

1 large onion, chopped
1 green chilli, finely chopped
½ inch piece of fresh root ginger,
  finely chopped
1 clove garlic, crushed
8 fl. oz. (1 cup) coconut milk (see
  page 10)
1 teaspoon curry powder

Cut the fish into 2 inch pieces. Place in a shallow dish with the lime juice, mustard, chilli powder and salt. Leave to marinate for 2-3 hours.

Drain the fish pieces, coat them with flour and fry in hot oil until golden brown on both sides.

Melt the butter in a frying pan (skillet), add the onion, chilli, ginger and garlic and fry until golden brown. Stir in the coconut milk and curry powder and bring to the boil, stirring. Then add the fried fish and simmer gently, uncovered, for 5 minutes.

Serves 4-6

Prawn (Shrimp) Curry

1 large onion, chopped
2 tablespoons (3T) oil
1½ oz. (½ cup) desiccated
  (shredded) coconut
½ teaspoon ground turmeric
1 teaspoon mustard seeds
½ teaspoon chilli powder
2 tablespoons (3T) natural
  (unflavored) yogurt

5 cloves garlic, crushed
½ teaspoon fenugreek
salt
few raisins (optional)
½ pint (1¼ cups) water
1 lb. (2⅔ cups) cooked shelled
  prawns (shrimp)
juice of ½ lemon

Fry the onion in the oil in a large frying pan (skillet) until it is golden brown. Then add all the remaining ingredients except the prawns and lemon juice. Cook for 10 minutes, stirring occasionally. Add the prawns and lemon juice and cook for a further 10 minutes.

Serve with plain boiled rice and a selection of side dishes, such as crushed pineapple, chutney, raisins and cucumber with yogurt.
Serves 4

Spiced Baked Cod

4 cod steaks
salt
juice of ½ lemon
5 fl. oz. (⅔ cup) natural
  (unflavored) yogurt
1 teaspoon garam masala

1 teaspoon cumin seeds, ground
¼ teaspoon chilli powder
2 cloves garlic, crushed
2 teaspoons vinegar
lemon wedges to garnish

Arrange the cod steaks in a shallow ovenproof dish and sprinkle with salt and lemon juice. Mix the yogurt with the spices, garlic and vinegar. Pour this mixture over the fish and leave in a cool place to marinate for about 4 hours.

Bake in a moderately hot oven, 375°F, Gas Mark 5 for 30 minutes. Garnish with lemon wedges before serving.
Serves 4

PRAWN (SHRIMP) CURRY WITH ACCOMPANIMENTS
(Photograph: Young's Seafood Ltd.)

CHICKEN

Chicken Korma Chicken Braised in Yogurt

1 ½ lb. chicken meat
3 onions
2 tablespoons (3T) oil
2 chillies
1 tablespoon ground cumin
1 teaspoon ground coriander
½ teaspoon ground turmeric
½ teaspoon ground ginger

½ teaspoon fenugreek
1 tablespoon desiccated
  (shredded) coconut
2 cardamoms, crushed
10 fl. oz. (1 ¼ cups) natural
  (unflavored) yogurt
salt
lemon wedges to garnish

Cut the chicken into 1 inch pieces. Thinly slice two of the onions. Heat the oil in a large pan, add the whole chillies and sliced onions and fry until brown.

Meanwhile, chop the remaining onion, then add it to the pan with all the spices, except the cardamoms. Stir in the coconut. Continue to fry until the spices darken in colour. Then add the chicken pieces, cardamoms and half of the yogurt. Simmer until the chicken is cooked, adding a little water if necessary and salt to taste.

When the chicken is cooked, stir in the remaining yogurt. Garnish with lemon wedges and serve with rice.

Serves 4

Chicken with Cashew Nuts

4 chicken joints
½ pint (1¼ cups) chicken stock
  (bouillon)
2 tablespoons (3T) oil
2 large onions, finely chopped
1 teaspoon chilli powder
2 cloves garlic, crushed
1 inch piece of fresh root ginger,
  finely chopped, or 1 teaspoon
  ground ginger

1 tablespoon curry powder
10 fl. oz. (1¼ cups) natural
  (unflavored) yogurt
4 oz. (1 cup) cashew nuts,
  chopped
salt

Put the chicken portions into a pan with the stock and simmer for about 45 minutes until tender. Then take out the chicken and set aside ¼ pint (⅔ cup) of the stock.

Heat the oil in a large, heavy frying pan (skillet) and fry the onions, chilli powder, garlic, ginger and curry powder until golden. Beat the yogurt with the reserved stock. Add the mixture to the pan and bring to the boil. Then add the chicken and simmer for a few minutes, stirring all the time. Stir in the cashew nuts and salt to taste.

Serve with rice and a selection of accompaniments.

Serves 4

Chicken and Lentil Curry

4 chicken joints, skinned
8 oz. (1 cup) lentils
1 pint (2½ cups) boiling water
2 onions, chopped
2 large potatoes, diced
2 tomatoes, skinned and chopped

1 aubergine (eggplant), chopped
2 tablespoons (3T) curry powder
juice of 1 lemon
1 teaspoon salt
2-3 sprigs of fresh mint

Wash the chicken joints and lentils and place them in a pan with the boiling water. Add the onions, potatoes, tomatoes and aubergine. Cook gently until the chicken is tender, about 45 minutes.

Remove the chicken and take the meat off the bone. Strain the contents of the pan through a sieve, pressing down the pulp with a spoon to extract the juices. Discard the residue and return the liquor to the pan with the chicken meat. Add the curry powder, lemon juice, salt and mint. Cook gently for a further 15 minutes.

Serve with a selection of accompaniments.

Serves 4

Chicken with Spiced Sauce

½ teaspoon ground coriander
½ teaspoon chilli powder
½ teaspoon garam masala
pinch of salt
juice of 1 lemon
4 chicken breasts
oil for shallow frying
Sauce:
10 fl. oz. (1¼ cups) natural
  (unflavored) yogurt

½ teaspoon ground ginger
1 teaspoon curry powder
1 tablespoon cayenne pepper
1 clove garlic, crushed
1 bay leaf
1 tablespoon tomato purée (paste)
grated rind of 1 lemon
Garnish:
parsley sprigs
lemon slices

Combine the coriander, chilli powder, garam masala, salt and lemon juice. Prick the chicken breasts all over with a fork and rub in the spice and lemon mixture. Leave to marinate for 4-5 hours.

Drain the chicken pieces and fry them in oil over moderate heat until they are brown all over and cooked through. Transfer to a serving dish and keep warm.

Meanwhile mix all the ingredients for the sauce and warm over a gentle heat, stirring constantly. Remove the bay leaf and pour the sauce over the chicken portions.

Garnish with parsley and lemon slices. Serve with pilau rice, grated coconut with sultanas (seedless white raisins) and a selection of other accompaniments.
Serves 4

Chicken Dopiazza

1½ lb. chicken meat
3 onions, thinly sliced
2 tablespoons (3T) oil
¼ teaspoon garlic powder
1 tablespoon coriander seeds
1 tablespoon ground cumin
½ teaspoon ground turmeric

1 teaspoon ground ginger
½-1 teaspoon chilli powder
freshly ground black pepper
salt
¾ lb. tomatoes, skinned and
  halved
¾ lb. small new potatoes, scraped

Cut the chicken into bite-sized pieces. Fry the onions in the oil in a large pan until they are golden brown. Mix the garlic with the spices and a little pepper. Add the spice mixture to the pan with the chicken meat. Fry, stirring all the time, for about 1 minute.

Pour in sufficient water to cover the meat and add salt to taste. Bring to the boil, cover and simmer for 45 minutes or until the chicken is nearly cooked. Add water during cooking, if necessary, to ensure the mixture does not become dry. Then add the tomatoes and potatoes and continue to simmer until the vegetables are cooked.
Serves 4

CHICKEN WITH SPICED SAUCE AND ACCOMPANIMENTS
(Photograph: Buxted Advisory Service)

Tandoori Tamatar
Tandoori Chicken in Tomato Sauce

2 lb. chicken
Marinade:
juice of 1 lemon
1 clove garlic, crushed
½ teaspoon ground coriander
½ teaspoon chilli powder
½ teaspoon fenugreek
1 teaspoon paprika
½ inch piece of fresh root ginger,
  finely chopped
½ teaspoon salt
freshly ground black pepper

2 tablespoons (3T) oil
Sauce:
2 oz. (¼ cup) butter
1 teaspoon salt
½ teaspoon sugar
1 lb. tomatoes, skinned and
  quartered
1 tablespoon garam masala
3 tablespoons (¼ cup) double
  (heavy) cream
Garnish:
chopped fresh parsley

Wash, skin and thoroughly dry the chicken. Cut it into 8 pieces. Make cuts all over the surface of the chicken. Mix the ingredients for the marinade and rub the mixture over the chicken pieces. Leave in a cool place for 4-5 hours, or overnight, to marinate.

Place the chicken pieces in a baking tin (pan) and baste with the oil. Cook in a moderately hot oven at 400°F, Gas Mark 6 for 30 minutes. Baste with the juices several times during cooking.

To make the sauce, melt the butter in a large frying pan (skillet) and add the salt, sugar and tomatoes. Cook, uncovered, for about 15 minutes, stirring occasionally. Place the mixture in an electric blender and emulsify for 30 seconds, or pass it through a sieve. Return the sauce to the pan and add the garam masala. Simmer for 10 minutes. Remove the pan from the heat and stir in the cream.

Add the cooked chicken pieces to the sauce and heat through but do not boil. Transfer to a warmed serving dish and sprinkle with chopped parsley.
Serves 4

Chicken Biryani Chicken with Rice

3 lb. chicken
1 tablespoon garam masala
salt
1 onion, chopped
¼ pint (⅔ cup) chicken stock
  (bouillon)
5 tablespoons (6T) natural
  (unflavored) yogurt

8 oz. (1⅓ cups) long-grain rice,
  soaked for 30 minutes in cold
  water
Garnish:
2 tomatoes, sliced
2 hard-boiled eggs, sliced
parsley sprigs

Wash, skin and cut the chicken into 8 pieces. Place the garam masala, 1 teaspoon salt and the onion in a large pan. Add the chicken pieces and the stock. Bring to the boil, then cover and simmer until the chicken is tender.

When cooked, remove the chicken from the pan. If desired, the meat may be removed from the bone. Place the chicken in a casserole.

Return the stock to the heat and mix in the yogurt. Boil the mixture until it is reduced by one third. Pour this liquid over the chicken pieces.

Meanwhile, drain the rice and cook in 1 pint (2½ cups) boiling salted water for 4 minutes, then drain thoroughly. Spread the partly cooked rice over the chicken mixture. Cover and cook in a moderate oven, 350°F, Gas Mark 4 for 30-40 minutes.

Garnish with slices of tomato, hard-boiled egg and sprigs of parsley.
Serves 4

Dry Chicken Curry with Yellow Rice

1 large onion, chopped
1 clove garlic, crushed
2 oz. (¼ cup) butter
2 teaspoons curry powder
2 teaspoons salt
1 teaspoon chilli powder
2½ lb. chicken, jointed
¼ pint (⅔ cup) water
1 lb. tomatoes
2 tablespoons (3T) natural
  (unflavored) yogurt

Yellow rice:
8 oz. (1⅓ cups) long-grain rice,
  soaked for 30 minutes in cold
  water
1 oz. (2T) butter
1 teaspoon ground turmeric
1 teaspoon cloves
1 teaspoon ground cumin
salt
1 pint (2½ cups) boiling water
small piece of cucumber, cut into
  strips

Sauté the onion and garlic gently in the butter in a large pan. Add the curry powder, salt, chilli powder and chicken. Fry, stirring occasionally, until the chicken joints are brown all over. Add the water, cover the pan and simmer for 45 minutes.

Drain the rice and fry in the butter in a large pan over moderate heat until it is golden and transparent. Add the turmeric, cloves, cumin and salt and mix well, then pour in the boiling water. Lower the heat and simmer, covered, for 15 minutes or until the rice is tender and the liquid absorbed. If wished, place the rice in an ovenproof dish and put into a warm oven for a few minutes to dry off. Add the cucumber strips.

Add the tomatoes and yogurt to the chicken and simmer for a further 5 minutes. Serve the chicken curry with the yellow rice, a bowl of salted peanuts and a dish of raw onion rings.

Serves 4

DRY CHICKEN CURRY WITH YELLOW RICE AND ACCOMPANIMENTS
(Photograph: The Rice Council)

Chicken Cider Curry

2 tablespoons (3T) oil
½ oz. (1T) butter
4 chicken joints
1 onion, sliced
1 apple, cored and sliced
1½ tablespoons (2T) curry
  powder
1 tablespoon cornflour
  (cornstarch)
¼ pint (⅔ cup) stock (bouillon)
¼ pint (⅔ cup) dry (hard) cider
salt and pepper
2 tablespoons (3T) sultanas
  (seedless white raisins)
2 tablespoons (3T) single (light)
  cream
few drops of lemon juice
parsley sprigs to garnish

Heat the oil and butter in a large pan over moderate heat. Fry the chicken joints until golden brown, then take them out and keep warm. Add the onion to the pan and cook gently until it is soft. Add the apple and continue cooking for 2-3 minutes. Then stir in the curry powder and cornflour. Blend in the stock and cider, season with salt and pepper and bring to the boil, stirring. Add the sultanas, cover the pan and simmer for 30 minutes.

Place the chicken joints on a warm serving dish. Add the cream and lemon juice to the sauce and pour it over the chicken. Garnish with parsley. Serve with pilau rice.

Serves 4

Chicken Kababs

3 lb. chicken
Marinade:
5 fl. oz. (⅔ cup) natural
  (unflavored) yogurt
1 clove garlic, crushed with a little
  salt
1 inch piece of fresh root ginger,
  very finely chopped
1 teaspoon ground coriander
1 teaspoon garam masala
2 teaspoons paprika
1 teaspoon chilli powder
juice of 1 lemon
Garnish:
lemon wedges
onion rings
tomato slices

Wash and skin the chicken and dry it thoroughly. Remove the meat from the bones and cut it into 2 inch cubes. Beat the yogurt and mix it with the other marinade ingredients to form a smooth paste. Thoroughly coat the chicken pieces with the mixture and leave to marinate in a cool place overnight.

Thread the chicken pieces onto skewers and grill (broil) for about 10 minutes, until the chicken is tender.

Garnish with lemon wedges, onion rings and tomato slices and serve with a salad and chappatis.

Serves 4-6

Tandoori Chicken

3 lb. oven ready chicken
salt
juice of 1 lime or lemon
5 fl. oz. (⅔ cup) natural
  (unflavored) yogurt
1 inch piece of fresh root ginger,
  finely chopped
1 clove garlic, crushed

¼ teaspoon chilli powder
3 tablespoons (¼ cup) oil
  (approximately)
½ teaspoon red food colouring
Garnish:
lemon wedges
onion rings

Remove the skin from the chicken. Make slits in the flesh and rub salt all over the chicken, then sprinkle with lime or lemon juice.

Beat the yogurt with the ginger, garlic and chilli powder. Then stir in 1 tablespoon of the oil and the food colouring. Spread this mixture all over the chicken and leave to marinate in the refrigerator for 12 hours.

Drain the chicken, reserving the marinade, and pour a little oil over it. Wrap the chicken in aluminium foil and roast it in a moderate oven, 350°F, Gas Mark 4, allowing 25 minutes per lb. About 15 minutes before the chicken is cooked, remove the foil, pour over a little more oil and baste with the marinade.

Garnish with lemon wedges and onion rings. Serve with pilau rice and a salad.
Serves 4-6

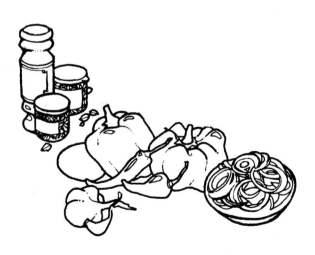

Chicken Curry

4 chicken joints, skinned
2 oz. (¼ cup) butter or ghee
1 onion, chopped
salt and pepper
2 tablespoons (3T) curry powder

1 tablespoon flour
¼ pint (⅔ cup) chicken stock
 (bouillon)
2 oz. (⅓ cup) sultanas (seedless
 white raisins)

Fry the chicken in the butter or ghee until it is lightly browned all over. Add the onion and fry until soft and transparent. Then add salt and pepper to taste and stir in the curry powder and flour. Cook for 1 minute, then blend in the stock. Add the sultanas and simmer, covered, for 30 minutes.

Serve on a bed of rice with pappadoms and a selection of side dishes, such as sliced bananas, chutney, grated coconut and sliced peppers.
Serves 4

Chicken Curry with Green Pepper

4 chicken joints
2 tablespoons (3T) oil
1 onion, chopped
1 green pepper, cored, seeded
 and sliced
2 tablespoons (3T) curry powder

1 tablespoon flour
1 pint (2½ cups) chicken stock
 (bouillon)
grated rind and juice of 1 lemon
salt and pepper

Lightly brown the chicken joints in the oil, then remove them from the pan and keep hot. Fry the onion and green pepper in the oil remaining in the pan until soft, then add the curry powder and flour and cook gently for 2 minutes, stirring. Blend in the stock, lemon rind and juice. Return the chicken to the pan and bring to the boil, stirring well. Add salt and pepper. Cover and simmer for 45 minutes.

Serve with rice and side dishes of tomato slices with onion rings, chutney and yogurt garnished with cucumber slices.
Serves 4

Chicken and Tomato Curry

3½ lb. chicken
6 onions, finely chopped
2 oz. (¼ cup) butter
2 teaspoons garam masala
5 fl. oz. (⅔ cup) natural
  (unflavored) yogurt

½ teaspoon salt
4 oz. (½ cup) tomatoes, peeled
  and chopped
¼ pint (⅔ cup) chicken stock
  (bouillon) or water

Wash and skin the chicken and cut it into 8 pieces. Fry the onions in the butter in a large pan until soft. Add the garam masala and yogurt and cook for a further 10 minutes. Then add the salt and tomatoes and cook over a low heat for a further 2-3 minutes. Add the chicken pieces and the stock or water. Cover and cook gently for 45 minutes or until the chicken is tender.

Serve with pilau rice and a selection of accompaniments.

Serves 4

Saffron Chicken

8 chicken drumsticks
salt
freshly ground black pepper
½ teaspoon saffron strands
1 tablespoon boiling water

3 tablespoons (¼ cup) ghee or oil
2 onions, finely chopped
2 cloves garlic, crushed
¼ teaspoon ground ginger
2 chillies, seeded and chopped

Season the chicken with salt and pepper. Soak the saffron strands in the boiling water. Heat the ghee or oil in a large pan and fry the chicken over moderate heat, turning occasionally, until evenly browned. Take out the chicken and set aside.

Add the onions, garlic, ginger and chillies to the oil remaining in the pan and sauté until the onions are soft and golden. Stir in the saffron and soaking liquor. Add the chicken and toss to coat thoroughly with the saffron mixture.

Cook over moderate heat, stirring frequently, for 15 minutes or until the chicken is tender. Add a little water during cooking, if the mixture becomes too dry.

Serve the chicken with rice or parathas and a selection of side dishes.

Serves 4

Mogul-Style Chicken

3 lb. chicken
3 cloves garlic, crushed
½ teaspoon ground ginger
1 teaspoon ground turmeric
½ teaspoon saffron strands
4 tablespoons (⅓ cup) hot milk
3 tablespoons (¼ cup) ghee or oil
3 onions, sliced

2 teaspoons garam masala
pinch of ground mace
salt
freshly ground black pepper
¼ pint (⅔ cup) chicken stock
 (bouillon)
1 oz. (¼ cup) ground almonds
¼ pint (⅔ cup) single (light) cream

Wash and skin the chicken. Cut into 8 serving pieces. Combine the garlic, ginger and turmeric and rub this mixture over the chicken pieces. Add the saffron to the hot milk and leave to soak for 10 minutes.

Meanwhile, heat the ghee or oil in a large flameproof casserole or heavy pan. Add the onions and sauté over moderate heat until softened and golden brown. Remove the onions with a slotted spoon and set aside.

Add the chicken pieces to the pan and fry, turning occasionally, until evenly browned. Sprinkle in the garam masala, mace and seasoning to taste. Stir in the stock, onions and saffron, together with the milk. Cover and simmer gently for 45 minutes or until the chicken is tender.

Transfer the chicken to a warm serving plate. Add the almonds and cream to the cooking liquor. Heat through gently, stirring constantly. Pour the sauce over the chicken. Serve with rice and a selection of accompaniments.
Serves 4

Chicken Vindaloo

2 oz. (¼ cup) butter
2 large onions, chopped
2 green chillies, finely chopped, or
  1 teaspoon chilli powder
2 cloves garlic, crushed
1 teaspoon ground ginger
2 tablespoons (3T) curry powder

2 tablespoons (3T) vinegar
½ pint (1¼ cups) water
4 chicken quarters, skinned
1 teaspoon salt
2 oz. (⅔ cup) desiccated
  (shredded) coconut

Melt the butter in a large pan and fry the onions, chillies and garlic. When the onions are golden brown, add the ginger and curry powder and cook gently for 2 minutes. Then add the vinegar, water and chicken joints. Bring to the boil, then cover and simmer gently for 30 minutes. Remove the lid and boil rapidly until the sauce thickens, then add the salt and coconut. Simmer for a further 15 minutes. Serve with a selection of accompaniments, including a dish of sliced banana, sliced pineapple and thinly sliced stem ginger.
Serves 4

Spicy Chicken

½ pint (1¼ cups) water
bouquet garni
1 small onion, sliced
1 carrot, sliced
salt
4 chicken joints

Spiced butter:
1 oz. (2T) butter
1 teaspoon curry powder
1 tablespoon peach chutney
squeeze of lemon juice
1 clove garlic, crushed

Put the water, bouquet garni, onion, carrot and a little salt into a large pan over moderate heat and bring to the boil. Add the chicken pieces and simmer for 20 minutes. Leave the chicken to cool in the liquid.

Mix together the ingredients for the spiced butter. Drain and dry the chicken portions and remove the skin, if preferred. Make several cuts in the chicken flesh with a knife and rub the spiced butter over the whole surface. Chill for a short time, then grill (broil) the chicken pieces until cooked through and golden brown all over.

Serve with pilau rice and a selection of accompaniments.
Serves 4

CHICKEN VINDALOO WITH ACCOMPANIMENT
(Photograph: RHM Foods Ltd.)

VEGETABLES

Vegetable Kofta Curry

¾ lb. potatoes
½ lb. (1½ cups) shelled peas
1 lb. (3 cups) carrots, sliced
salt and pepper
flour for coating
oil for deep frying
3 onions, finely chopped
2 oz. (¼ cup) ghee or butter
1 clove garlic, crushed
1 inch piece of fresh root ginger,
  finely chopped

1 tablespoon ground turmeric
1 teaspoon ground cinnamon
1 teaspoon ground cloves
2 tomatoes, skinned and mashed
½ pint (1¼ cups) vegetable stock
  (bouillon)
¼ teaspoon chilli powder
4 tablespoons (⅓ cup) double
  (heavy) cream
chopped coriander leaves to
  garnish

Cook the potatoes, peas and carrots separately in boiling salted water until tender. Mash the cooked vegetables together and season to taste with salt and pepper. Form the mixture into small balls and coat them with flour. Fry in the hot oil until golden brown. Remove and drain on kitchen paper.

Fry the onions in the ghee or butter until golden brown. Add the garlic, ginger, turmeric, cinnamon, cloves and a little water. Cook for 2 minutes. Add the tomatoes and simmer until the mixture forms a thick sauce. Then add the stock, salt, pepper and chilli powder and bring to the boil. Place the cooked koftas in the sauce and simmer for 15 minutes. Add the cream just before serving and garnish with chopped coriander leaves.

Serves 6

Bhujiya

2 onions, chopped
4 tablespoons (⅓ cup) oil
1 aubergine (eggplant), diced
3 medium potatoes, diced
½ teaspoon ground ginger
½ teaspoon ground turmeric
¼ teaspoon chilli powder
¼ teaspoon garam masala
pinch of cayenne pepper
3 tomatoes, skinned and chopped
½ pint (1 ¼ cups) water
pinch of salt

Fry the onions in the oil until they are golden brown. Then add the aubergine, potatoes and the spices. Stir and continue to fry until the spices turn brown. Add the tomatoes, water and salt. Cover and cook gently, stirring frequently, until the vegetables are cooked and the liquid has been absorbed. Add a little more liquid if the vegetables become too dry during cooking.
Serves 4

Sabzi Ka Curry Vegetable Curry

4 potatoes, diced
4 carrots, diced
¼ small turnip, diced
4 oz. (¾ cup) shelled peas
4 oz. (½ cup) runner beans, chopped
1 large onion, finely chopped
1 tablespoon oil
1 clove garlic, crushed
1 tablespoon ground coriander
1 teaspoon ground turmeric
1 teaspoon ground ginger
1 teaspoon chilli powder
½ teaspoon ground cumin
2 tablespoons (3T) tomato purée (paste)
1 tablespoon desiccated (shredded) coconut
salt
1-2 teaspoons lemon juice

Parboil the potatoes, carrots, turnip, peas and beans together in boiling salted water for 5 minutes. Drain the vegetables and reserve the cooking liquid.

Fry the onion in the oil until golden brown, then add the garlic. Mix the spices together and stir them into the oil. Cook for 2 minutes. Add the tomato puree and enough of the reserved liquid to make a thick gravy. Lower the heat, cover the pan and simmer gently for 10 minutes.

Stir in the coconut, parboiled vegetables and salt to taste. Cover the pan and continue to simmer until the vegetables are tender. Add lemon juice to taste.

Serve as a main-course dish in addition to meat curries or on its own with rice and dhal.
Serves 4

Gobi Dhal Curry Cauliflower and Lentil Curry

4 oz. (½ cup) lentils
2 onions, chopped
1 tablespoon oil
2 tablespoons (3T) curry powder
1 tablespoon flour
1 pint (2½ cups) chicken stock
  (bouillon)
2 oz. (¼ cup) salted peanuts

1 oz. (⅓ cup) desiccated
  (shredded) coconut
2 tablespoons (3T) mango
  chutney
1 medium cauliflower, divided
  into florets
juice of ½ lemon
salt and pepper

Place the lentils in a pan and pour over sufficient cold water to cover. Bring to the boil and simmer for 5 minutes, then drain.

Fry the onions in the oil until softened. Stir in the curry powder and flour and cook gently for 2 minutes. Add the stock, peanuts, coconut, chutney and drained lentils. Bring to the boil, cover and simmer for 15 minutes.

Stir in the cauliflower, lemon juice and a little salt and pepper. Simmer, covered, for 20-25 minutes. Serve with plain boiled rice and a selection of accompaniments.
Serves 4

Gobi Curry Cauliflower Curry

1 onion, finely chopped
1 oz. (2T) butter or ghee
½ teaspoon dry mustard
1 teaspoon ground turmeric
¼ teaspoon garlic powder
½ teaspoon ground ginger

½ teaspoon chilli powder
salt
1 medium cauliflower, divided
  into florets
1 teaspoon garam masala

Fry the onion in the butter or ghee until it is golden brown. Add all the spices, except the garam masala. Add salt to taste, stir well and cook for 2 minutes. Then add the cauliflower and 3 tablespoons (¼ cup) water. Cook, covered, over low heat. When the cauliflower is just tender, sprinkle in the garam masala and cook for a further 5 minutes.
Serves 4

Lentil Curry

1 lb. (2 cups) lentils
1 teaspoon salt
1 pint (2½ cups) water
2 onions
½ teaspoon ground turmeric
1 oz. (2T) butter or ghee
2 red chillies, finely chopped

½ teaspoon cumin seeds
5 cloves garlic, crushed
1 inch piece of fresh root ginger,
  finely chopped
2 tomatoes, skinned and chopped
chopped coriander leaves to
  garnish

Place the lentils, salt and water in a large pan. Bring to the boil. Chop one of the onions and add it to the pan with the turmeric. Cover and cook for 20 minutes, or until the lentils are tender.

Slice the remaining onion and sauté in the butter or ghee until golden brown. Mix the spices to a paste with the garlic and ginger and add to the onion. Fry for 2-3 minutes, stirring, then add the spiced mixture to the lentils. Add the tomatoes and simmer until they are cooked.

Serve garnished with chopped coriander leaves.

Serves 6-8

Kabli Channas Chick Peas (Garbanzos)

1½ lb. (3½ cups) chick peas
  (garbanzos), soaked for 6-8
  hours in cold water
1 inch piece of fresh root ginger
½ teaspoon ground cloves
1 green chilli
10 peppercorns
2 cloves garlic
½ teaspoon ground cinnamon

½ teaspoon ground turmeric
2 large onions, chopped
2 oz. (¼ cup) butter or ghee
3 tomatoes, skinned and mashed
½ pint (1¼ cups) vegetable stock
  (bouillon)
chopped coriander leaves to
  garnish

Drain the chick peas and cook in boiling salted water for about 45 minutes. Drain thoroughly. Using an electric grinder or a pestle and mortar, grind together the ginger, cloves, chilli, peppercorns, garlic, cinnamon and turmeric to form a smooth paste.

Fry the onions in the butter or ghee until golden. Add the spice paste to the onions, stir and cook gently for 3-4 minutes. Then add the tomato pulp and the chick peas. Cook, stirring, for 5 minutes. Then pour in the stock and bring to the boil. Cover the pan and simmer over low heat for 20 minutes.

Garnish with chopped coriander leaves and serve with rice or chappatis.

Serves 4

Sag Paneer Spinach and Cottage Cheese

2 oz. (¼ cup) butter or ghee
½ teaspoon ground turmeric
1 teaspoon ground coriander
1 teaspoon salt

1 ¼ lb. frozen spinach, broken up
4 oz. (½ cup) cottage cheese
1 tablespoon soured cream

Melt the butter or ghee in a pan and stir in the spices and salt. Cook over low heat, stirring, for about 5 minutes. Then add the spinach, cover the pan and cook over moderate heat until the spinach is hot.

Combine the cottage cheese and soured cream in a bowl and beat thoroughly. Add this mixture to the hot spinach. Cook, stirring, until the mixture is thoroughly blended.
Serves 8

Aubergine (Eggplant) Fritters

2 tablespoons (3T) gram flour
1 teaspoon salt
24 coriander seeds
¼ teaspoon ground turmeric

2 aubergines (eggplants), cut into
  ¼ inch slices
oil for deep frying

Mix the flour, salt and spices in a bowl and stir in enough water to form a thick batter of a consistency similar to porridge. Dip the aubergine slices in the batter and deep fry them in the hot oil until golden brown. Drain on kitchen paper. Serve hot.
Serves 4-6

Mixed Vegetable Cutlets

1 lb. potatoes
½ lb. (1 ½ cups) carrots, sliced
4 oz. (½ cup) French (green)
  beans, chopped
2 oz. (⅓ cup) shelled peas
1 onion, finely chopped
1 clove garlic, crushed
1 inch piece of fresh root ginger,
  finely chopped

few coriander leaves, finely
  chopped
salt and pepper
3 oz. (¾ cup) gram flour
  (approximately)
oil for deep frying

Cook the potatoes, carrots, beans and peas, separately, in boiling salted water until tender. Then drain thoroughly. Mash the potatoes and combine with the other cooked vegetables. Add the onion, garlic, ginger, coriander leaves and salt and pepper to taste. Mix well, then stir in 2 oz. (½ cup) of the flour to thicken. Shape into small cutlets or rounds, each weighing about 2 oz.. Coat the cutlets with flour and deep fry in the hot oil until golden brown.
Serves 4-6

MEAT

Madras Meat Curry

2 onions, thinly sliced
2 tablespoons (3T) oil
2 cardamoms, crushed
1 tablespoon corainder seeds,
  crushed
1 tablespoon ground cumin
1 tablespoon ground turmeric
1 teaspoon chilli powder

2 cloves garlic, crushed
1 lb. lean lamb or beef, cut into
  1 inch cubes
1 pint (2½ cups) stock (bouillon)
2 bay leaves
salt
freshly ground black pepper
juice of ½ lemon

Fry the onions in the oil until golden brown, then take out of the pan and set aside. Mix all the spices with the garlic. Rub the spice mixture into the meat. Add to the pan and fry until the spice coating turns a rich brown colour.

Return the onions to the pan and add the stock and bay leaves. Bring to the boil, add salt and pepper to taste and simmer, covered, until the meat is tender, about 1¼ hours. Make sure the sauce does not boil dry. Just before serving remove the bay leaves and add the lemon juice.

Serve with rice and a selection of accompaniments, including pappadoms.
Serves 4

Dry Lamb with Ginger

1 onion, chopped
1 tablespoon oil
1 tablespoon curry powder
1 lb. lean lamb, trimmed and cut
  into 1 inch cubes
2 teaspoons vinegar

1 tablespoon tomato purée (paste)
1 inch piece of fresh root ginger,
  finely chopped
salt and pepper
1 tablespoon desiccated
  (shredded) coconut

Fry the onion in the oil until it is golden. Stir in the curry powder and cook gently for 2 minutes. Add the meat and brown lightly. Stir in the vinegar, tomato purée, ginger and a little salt and pepper. Stir well, bring to the boil, cover and simmer gently, stirring occasionally to prevent the ingredients sticking to the pan. If the mixture becomes too dry, add a little water. Cook until the meat is tender, about 1 hour, add the coconut and stir briskly.

Serve with rice and a selection of accompaniments.
Serves 4

MADRAS MEAT CURRY WITH PAPPADOMS

Boti Kabab Grilled Meat on Skewers

¼ pint (⅔ cup) natural
  (unflavored) yogurt
2 teaspoons ground coriander
1 teaspoon black pepper
½ teaspoon ground turmeric
1 teaspoon chilli powder

salt
1½ lb. lean lamb, cut into 1 inch
  cubes
6 small onions
lemon wedges to garnish

Beat the yogurt and mix in the spices and salt to taste. Mix in the cubes of meat and leave to marinate overnight.

Cut the onions into quarters and separate each layer of onion. Thread the onion pieces and meat alternately onto skewers. Grill (broil) for about 5 minutes on each side.

Garnish with lemon wedges and serve with rice, chappatis and relishes.
Serves 4-6

Lamb or Mutton Curry

1 oz. (¼ cup) coriander seeds
3 onions
3 cloves garlic
1 oz. (¼ cup) ground almonds
salt
1½ lb. lean lamb or mutton, cut
  into 1 inch cubes
1 oz. (2T) ghee or butter
¼ pint (⅔ cup) hot water

5 fl. oz. (⅔ cup) natural
  (unflavored) yogurt
¼ pint (⅔ cup) single (light) cream
pinch of ground saffron
½ teaspoon curry powder
1 teaspoon paprika
juice of 1 lemon
chopped coriander leaves to
  garnish

Pass the coriander seeds, two of the onions and the garlic through a mincer (grinder), then mix to a paste with the almonds, adding salt to taste. Spread this paste over the meat and leave it to marinate for 2 hours.

Heat the ghee or butter in a large pan. Slice the remaining onion, add to the pan and sauté until softened. Then take out the onion and add the marinated meat to the pan. Fry for 2-3 minutes, stirring. Add the hot water and simmer, covered, over low heat for 20 minutes. Then remove the lid and continue cooking until the liquor has reduced and the mixture is quite dry. Stir occasionally to prevent the meat sticking to the pan.

Beat the yogurt and add it to the meat, then continue cooking, uncovered, for 5 minutes. Add the fried onion. Beat the cream, mix in the saffron and add to the meat. Then mix in the curry powder, paprika and lemon juice.

Transfer to a casserole, cover and cook in a moderate oven at 325°F, Gas Mark 3 for 30 minutes. Serve the curry on a bed of rice with pappadoms, cucumber with yogurt and mango chutney.
Serves 4-6

Shami Kabab

2 oz. (¼ cup) chick peas
 (garbanzos)
1 lb. lean lamb or beef, cut into
 ½ inch cubes
½ pint (1 ¼ cups) stock (bouillon)
¼ teaspoon chilli powder
¼ teaspoon ground turmeric
¼ teaspoon ground cumin
¼ teaspoon ground cinnamon
salt and pepper
1 inch piece of fresh root ginger,
 finely chopped

2 cloves garlic, crushed
1 small onion, finely chopped
¼ teaspoon grated lemon rind
few coriander leaves, finely
 chopped
2 eggs, beaten
flour for coating
oil for deep frying
Garnish:
onion rings
tomato slices
cucumber slices

Wash the chick peas and soak them in cold water for 2 hours. Drain the chick peas and place them in a pan with the meat and stock. Bring to the boil, then cover and simmer until the chick peas and meat are tender and the liquid is absorbed.

Pass the cooked meat and chick peas through a mincer (grinder) with the spices and salt and pepper to taste. Then mix in the ginger, garlic, onion, lemon rind and coriander leaves. Mix with enough beaten egg to bind, then divide the mixture into 16 balls.

Dredge the meat balls with flour and deep fry them in the hot oil until golden brown. Garnish with onion rings, tomato slices and cucumber slices.

Serves 4

Sag Gosht Beef and Spinach Curry

1 oz. (2T) butter or ghee
1 tablespoon oil
2 onions, finely chopped
1 clove garlic, crushed
1 inch piece of fresh root ginger,
  finely chopped
1 teaspoon ground turmeric
½ teaspoon chilli powder

1 tablespoon ground coriander
1 teaspoon ground mustard seeds
1½-2 lb. stewing steak, cut into
  1 inch cubes
8 oz. packet frozen spinach,
  thawed and drained
10 fl. oz. (1¼ cups) natural
  (unflavored) yogurt

Heat the butter or ghee and oil in a large pan. Add the onions, garlic and spices and fry over gentle heat until the onions are soft. Add the meat and fry, stirring occasionally, until evenly browned.

Stir in the spinach and half of the yogurt. Cover and simmer over low heat for 2 hours or until the meat is tender. Add a little water during cooking if the curry becomes dry.

Before serving, add the remaining yogurt. Serve with plain boiled rice, parathas and mango chutney.
Serves 4

Seekh Kabab

1 lb. (2 cups) minced (ground)
  lamb or beef
2 onions, finely chopped
½ inch piece of fresh root ginger,
  very finely chopped
2 cloves garlic, crushed
¼ teaspoon ground cardamom
¼ teaspoon ground cumin
¼ teaspoon ground cloves

1 teaspoon ground coriander
salt
1 egg, beaten
1 tablespoon oil
Garnish:
lemon slices
tomato slices
chopped coriander leaves or
  chopped fresh parsley

Mix the meat with the onions, ginger and garlic. Mix the ground spices with salt to taste and stir into the meat mixture with enough beaten egg to bind. Divide the mixture into 8 balls.

Flatten the meat balls to form sausage shapes then thread these onto skewers. Brush with oil and place under a hot grill (broil). Cook, turning the kababs occasionally, until the meat is tender.

Garnish with lemon and tomato slices and sprinkle with chopped coriander or chopped parsley. Serve with boiled or fried rice, salad and a selection of accompaniments.
Serves 4

Roghan Gosht Beef and Onion Curry

1 oz. (2T) butter or ghee
2 large onions, finely chopped
1 clove garlic, crushed
1 teaspoon finely chopped fresh
  root ginger or ½ teaspoon
  ground ginger
1½-2 lb. chuck steak, cut into
  1 inch cubes
1 tablespoon ground turmeric
1 tablespoon ground coriander

1 teaspoon ground cumin
½ teaspoon chilli powder
salt
freshly ground black pepper
2 oz. can tomato purée (paste)
½ pint (1¼ cups) beef stock
  (bouillon)
8 oz. (1⅓ cups) long-grain rice
4 orange or lemon wedges

Melt the butter or ghee in a flameproof casserole or heavy pan over
moderate heat. Add the onions, garlic and ginger and sauté gently until the
onions are soft. Add the meat, remaining spices and seasoning to taste.
Continue frying, stirring occasionally, until the meat is evenly browned.

Stir in the tomato purée and beef stock and bring to the boil. Lower the
heat, cover and simmer for 2 hours or until the meat is tender.

Meanwhile, soak the rice in cold water for 30 minutes. Then drain and
cook in boiling salted water until just tender. Drain thoroughly and arrange
around the edge of a warm serving dish. Spoon the curry into the centre of
the dish.

Garnish with orange or lemon wedges and serve with a selection of side
dishes such as cucumber with yogurt, mango chutney and tomato and
banana salad.

Serves 4

Keema Pimento
Minced Meat with Green Pepper

1 green pepper, cored, seeded
  and cut into strips
3 tablespoons (¼ cup) oil
2 onions, chopped
1 teaspoon salt
1 teaspoon freshly ground black
  pepper
½ teaspoon ground cumin

2 teaspoons garam masala
¼ teaspoon ground cinnamon
1 teaspoon chilli powder
1½ lb. (3 cups) minced (ground)
  beef or lamb
stock or water (optional)
green pepper slices to garnish

Fry the strips of green pepper in the oil for about 1 minute. Then take them out of the pan with a slotted spoon. Fry the onions in the oil remaining in the pan until golden brown. Mix the salt and pepper with the spices and add to the onions. Cook for 2 minutes, stirring all the time.

Add the minced meat and cook over low heat, stirring occasionally, to make sure it does not stick to the pan. Add a little stock or water, if necessary. Cook for about 20 minutes, then add the green pepper and continue cooking for 10 minutes.

Garnish with green pepper slices. Serve with rice and a selection of accompaniments such as peach chutney and mango chutney.
Serves 4-6

Pork Vindaloo
Very Hot Spiced Pork

1 lb. belly of pork (fatty unsmoked
  bacon slices), cut into 1 inch
  pieces
Marinade:
1 clove garlic, crushed
1 tablespoon ground cumin
2 teaspoons chilli powder
2 teaspoons ground coriander

½ teaspoon ground ginger
¼ pint (⅔ cup) malt vinegar

1 large onion, chopped
8 whole chillies
3 tablespoons (¼ cup) oil
½ teaspoon ground turmeric
salt

Place the meat in a deep dish. Mix the marinade ingredients and pour the mixture over the meat. Leave to marinate for several hours, stirring occasionally.

Fry the onion and chillies in the oil until brown. Then add the turmeric and continue to fry for 1 minute. Pour in the meat and marinade mixture, add salt to taste and simmer, covered, until the meat is tender, about 1¼ hours. Add water, as necessary, to give a thin sauce.

Serve with boiled or fried rice and a selection of accompaniments.
Serves 4

Koftas Meat Balls

Koftas:
1½ lb. (3 cups) finely minced
  (ground) meat
2 onions, finely chopped or
  coarsely grated
2 oz. (1 cup) fresh breadcrumbs
2 green chillies, finely chopped
freshly ground black pepper
pinch of ground cinnamon
pinch of ground cloves
1 egg, beaten
oil for deep frying

Sauce:
1 oz. (2T) ghee or butter
1 oz. (¼ cup) flour
1-2 teaspoons curry powder
½ pint (1¼ cups) white stock
  (bouillon)
¼ pint (⅔ cup) single (light) cream
Garnish:
sliced tomato
sliced green pepper

Mix the meat with the rest of the kofta ingredients, adding enough beaten egg to bind. Form the mixture into small balls and deep fry them in the hot oil until golden brown. Drain on kitchen paper.

To make the sauce, melt the fat in a large pan. Blend in the flour and curry powder and cook for 1-2 minutes. Stir in the stock and bring to the boil, stirring. Cook gently, stirring until the sauce has thickened. Add the cream and seasoning.

Place the meat balls in the sauce and simmer gently for 10 minutes. Shake the pan occasionally to make sure they do not stick or burn.

Serve the meat balls and sauce on a bed of plain boiled rice. Garnish with sliced tomato and green pepper.
Serves 4-6

Mild Pork and Apple Curry

1 onion, chopped
4 tablespoons (⅓ cup) oil
4 teaspoons curry powder
2 tablespoons (3T) flour
1 lb. lean pork, cut into 1 inch
  cubes

½ pint (1¼ cups) stock (bouillon)
1 apple, cored and finely chopped
1 teaspoon salt
juice of ½ lemon

Fry the onion in the oil until it is transparent. Stir in the curry powder and flour and cook gently for 2 minutes. Add the meat and brown it lightly. Then mix in the stock, apple and salt. Bring to the boil, reduce heat, cover the pan and simmer gently for 1 hour or until the meat is tender. Add the lemon juice just before removing the pan from the heat.
Serves 4

SIDE DISHES AND CHUTNEYS

Brinjal Bhartha

4-5 aubergines (eggplants)
6 tablespoons (½ cup) oil
  (approximately)
1 green chilli
10 peppercorns
2 cloves garlic
½ teaspoon ground turmeric
3 onions, chopped

small piece of fresh root ginger,
  chopped
4 tomatoes, skinned and mashed
¼ teaspoon chilli powder
salt and pepper
chopped coriander leaves to
  garnish

Baste the aubergines with a little oil and bake them in a moderate oven at 350°F, Gas Mark 4 for about 45 minutes, or until tender. When cool, remove the skins and mash the pulp.

Using an electric grinder or pestle and mortar, grind the chilli, peppercorns, garlic and turmeric together to form a paste. Heat 5 tablespoons (6T) oil in a large frying pan (skillet) and sauté the onions until golden brown in colour. Add the spice paste to the onions with the ginger and cook for 2 minutes, stirring.

Add the mashed aubergines and cook until slightly browned, stirring well. Add the tomatoes, chilli powder and season to taste with salt and pepper. Cover and cook for 15 minutes over low heat. Chill before serving and garnish with coriander leaves.
Serves 8

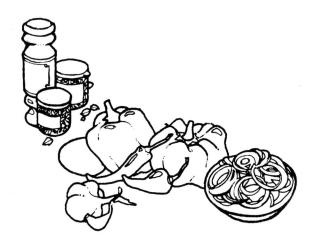

Fresh Cucumber Chutney

1 cucumber
juice of ½ lemon
¼ teaspoon chilli powder

few drops of vinegar
salt to taste

Peel the cucumber and slice it very thinly. Mix the lemon juice, chilli powder, vinegar and salt and sprinkle the mixture over the cucumber. Chill before serving.
Serve 6

Fresh Onion Chutney

3 onions, thinly sliced
salt
½ teaspoon chilli powder

few drops of vinegar or lemon
juice

Sprinkle the sliced onions with salt and leave for 3-4 minutes, then rinse and drain. Add the chilli powder, a few drops of vinegar or lemon juice and salt to taste. Toss the onions to coat thoroughly.
Serves 6-8

Pudinha Chutney Mint Chutney

8 oz. fresh mint leaves
6 spring onions (scallions)
2 green chillies, seeded
1 inch piece of fresh root ginger,
  finely chopped

1 tablespoon pomegranate seeds
3 tablespoons (¼ cup) lime juice
1 tablespoon sugar

Wash and dry the mint leaves. Put them through a mincer (grinder) with the spring onions (scallions) and green chillies. Add the ginger and pomegranate seeds and mince (grind) again. Combine the lime juice and sugar and add to the mint mixture. Toss to coat thoroughly.
Serves 10

Spiced Fruit and Vegetables

1 onion, chopped
4 celery stalks, chopped
1 tablespoon oil
1 tablespoon curry powder
1 tablespoon flour
½ pint (1¼ cups) light stock
  (bouillon) or water
1 inch piece of fresh root ginger,
  finely chopped, or 1 teaspoon
  ground ginger

juice and grated rind of 1 lemon
14 oz. can apricot halves, drained
2 bananas, peeled and thickly
  sliced
1 lb. cooking apples, peeled,
  cored and quartered
4 oz. (⅔ cup) raisins
¼ pint (⅔ cup) soured cream

Fry the onion and celery in the oil until golden. Stir in the curry powder and flour and cook gently for 2-3 minutes, stirring constantly. Mix the stock or water with the ginger and gradually stir into the pan. Add the lemon juice, rind, apricots, bananas, apples and raisins. Stir well and cook, covered, over low heat until the fruit is tender. Just before serving, stir in the soured cream.
Serves 6

Cauliflower Pickle

1 medium cauliflower, divided
  into florets
2 tablespoons (3T) salt
2 teaspoons ground turmeric
2 teaspoons chilli powder

1 tablespoon black mustard seeds,
  crushed
2 teaspoons garam masala
5 oz. (½ cup) fresh root ginger,
  sliced

Place the cauliflower in a pan and pour over sufficient water to cover. Bring to the boil, then drain and cool. Place the cauliflower sprigs in a large glass jar and add the remaining ingredients. Cover with a lid and shake well.

Keep the covered jar of pickle in a warm cupboard or in the sun for a few days before using it. Thereafter, store in a cool place.
Makes about 2 lb.

Variation:
To make sweet pickle, follow the above recipe but soak 2 oz. dried tamarind in ¼ pint (⅔ cup) boiling water. Strain through a piece of muslin or cheesecloth into a cup, squeezing well to press out the tamarind juice. Add the tamarind liquid to the prepared pickle. Mix 3 tablespoons (¼ cup) vinegar with 4 oz. (⅔ cup) brown sugar in a small pan. Boil the mixture for 2-3 minutes then add to the pickle. Shake well.

Banana Raita Banana with Yogurt

3 bananas, sliced
1 tablespoon lemon juice
5 fl. oz. (⅔ cup) natural
 (unflavored) yogurt

1 tablespoon desiccated
 (shredded) coconut

Sprinkle the bananas with the lemon juice, then toss them in the yogurt.
Top with coconut and serve immediately.
Serves 6

Alu Raita Potatoes in Yogurt

½ lb. potatotes
salt
1 ¼ pints (3 cups) natural
 (unflavored) yogurt
1 teaspoon cumin seeds

¼ teaspoon chilli powder
freshly ground black pepper
chopped coriander leaves to
 garnish

Cook the potatoes in boiling salted water until just tender. Drain and cool,
then dice the potatoes.

Whisk the yogurt in a bowl with the cumin seeds, chilli powder and salt
and pepper to taste. Chill and mix in the potatoes just before serving.
Garnish with chopped coriander leaves.
Serves 4

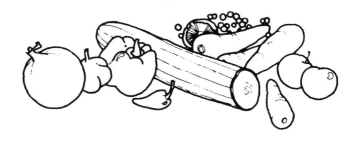

Yogurt Salad

2 tomatoes, skinned and chopped
¼ cucumber, peeled and sliced
few spring onions (scallions),
  chopped
few radishes, sliced

10 fl. oz. (1 ¼ cups) natural
  (unflavored) yogurt
pinch of salt
pinch of chilli powder
paprika to garnish

Place all the ingredients except the paprika in a bowl and mix well. Chill
and sprinkle with paprika before serving.
Serves 4

Kutchumber Mixed Salad

½ cucumber, peeled and sliced
2 onions, sliced
3 tomatoes, sliced
½ lettuce, shredded
2 teaspoons vinegar

2 teaspoons lime juice
salt and pepper
pinch of chilli powder
chopped coriander leaves to
  garnish

Combine the cucumber, onions, tomatoes and lettuce in a bowl. Mix the
vinegar with the lime juice, salt and pepper to taste, and chilli powder. Toss
the salad in this mixture. Sprinkle with chopped coriander leaves to
garnish.
Serves 4

Cucumber Raita Cucumber with Yogurt

5 fl. oz. (⅔ cup) natural
  (unflavored) yogurt
1 cucumber, cut into thin strips

1 onion, finely chopped
chilli powder to taste

Mix the yogurt with the cucumber and onion, then sprinkle over a little
chilli powder. Chill before serving.
Serves 4-6

Coconut Chutney

flesh of 1 coconut
1 red chilli
1 inch piece of fresh root ginger

2 onions, roughly chopped
1 inch piece of tamarind, soaked in
 a little boiling water

Put all the ingredients except the tamarind through a mincer (grinder).
Squeeze the tamarind in a piece of muslin or cheesecloth to extract the
juice, then add the liquid to the other ingredients. Mix well.
Serves 10

Coriander Chutney

1 bunch coriander leaves
1 green chilli
4 oz. (1⅓ cups) fresh, grated, or
 desiccated (shredded) coconut
3 cloves garlic

2 onions, sliced
1 inch piece of fresh root ginger
½ teaspoon ground cumin
juice of ¼ lime
1 teaspoon sugar

Wash and dry the coriander leaves. Pass all the ingredients except the lime
juice and sugar through a mincer (grinder). Mix the lime juice with the
sugar and combine with the other ingredients.
Serves 4

Tomato Sambal

4 tomatoes, skinned and cut into
 wedges
1 onion, finely chopped
1 tablespoon lemon juice

pinch of sugar
½ teaspoon salt
chopped fresh parsley to garnish

Mix the tomatoes and onion in a serving bowl. Blend the lemon juice with
the sugar and salt and sprinkle over the tomatoes and onion. Garnish with
chopped parsley.
Serves 4

RICE

Kashmiri Pilau

1 lb. (2⅔ cups) long-grain rice
3 oz. (⅓ cup) ghee or butter
5 whole cardamoms
5 bay leaves
½ stick cinnamon
8 whole cloves
1 teaspoon cumin seeds

2 pints (5 cups) vegetable stock
  (bouillon) or water
salt
Garnish:
1 oz. (¼ cup) slivered almonds
1 oz. (¼ cup) walnut halves
fried onion rings

Wash the rice, soak in cold water for 30 minutes, then drain thoroughly.

Heat the ghee or butter in a large pan and sauté the cardamoms, bay leaves, cinnamon, cloves and cumin seeds until slightly brown. Add the drained rice and cook until the grains are transparent, stirring to prevent it sticking to the pan.

Add the stock or water with salt to taste. Bring to the boil, then cover and simmer until the rice is cooked and the liquid is absorbed. If preferred, cook the rice in a moderate oven at 325°F, Gas Mark 3 until tender.

Dry the rice, uncovered, in the oven. Garnish with almonds, walnuts and onion rings before serving.
Serves 8

Fried Rice

8 oz. (1⅓ cups) long-grain rice
3 oz. (⅓ cup) butter or ghee
2 onions, finely chopped
1 teaspoon sugar
12 cardamoms crushed

4-6 black peppercorns, crushed
2 teaspoons ground cinnamon
2 teaspoons ground cloves
1 pint (2½ cups) water
1 teaspoon salt

Wash the rice, soak for 30 minutes in cold water, then drain thoroughly.

Heat the butter or ghee in a large pan and fry the onions until they are soft and lightly coloured. Then add the sugar and spices and cook for 1 minute, stirring.

Stir in the rice and cook until the grains are transparent. Then add the water and salt. Bring to the boil, cover and simmer until the rice is cooked and the liquid is absorbed. Dry the rice, uncovered, in a moderate oven, 325°F, Gas Mark 3 until the grains are separate.
Serves 4

Peas Pilau

1 lb. (2⅔ cups) long-grain rice
3 oz. (⅓ cup) ghee or butter
2 onions, sliced into rings
1 teaspoon cloves
1 teaspoon ground cinnamon or
  small piece of cinnamon

5 bay leaves
½ lb. (1½ cups) shelled peas
2 pints (5 cups) vegetable stock
  (bouillon) or water
salt and pepper
¼ teaspoon chilli powder

Wash the rice and soak for 30 minutes in cold water, then drain thoroughly.

Heat the ghee or butter in a large pan and fry the onion rings until they are golden brown. Add the cloves, cinnamon and bay leaves. Cook, stirring, for 1 minute.

Stir in the rice and cook until the grains are transparent. Add the peas and continue cooking, stirring, for 1 minute. Then add the stock or water with salt and pepper to taste and the chilli powder. Bring to the boil and simmer, covered, until the rice and peas are cooked and the liquid is absorbed. If preferred, the cooking can be done in a moderate oven at 325°F, Gas Mark 3.

Dry the rice, uncovered, in a moderate oven until the grains are separate.
Serves 8-10

Turmeric Rice

1 lb. (2⅔ cups) long-grain rice
salt
2 pints (5 cups) water

1 teaspoon ground turmeric
pinch of chilli powder
1 bay leaf

Wash the rice and soak it in cold water for about 30 minutes. Drain thoroughly.

Cook the rice in boiling salted water, with the spices and bay leaf added, until just tender, about 15 minutes. Dry the rice, uncovered in a moderate oven, 325°F, Gas Mark 3 until the grains are separate and fluffy.
Serves 8

Pilau Rice

8 oz. (1⅓ cups) long-grain rice
1 onion, chopped
3 oz. (⅓ cup) butter or ghee
4 whole cardamoms
1 stick of cinnamon

5-6 whole cloves
½ teaspoon ground turmeric
4 bay leaves
1 pint (2½ cups) water
1 teaspoon salt

Wash the rice and soak it in cold water for about 1 hour. Drain thoroughly.

Fry the onion in the butter or ghee until it is golden brown, then add the spices and bay leaves and fry for 2 minutes. Stir in the drained rice and fry for a further 2 minutes. Add the water and salt and bring to the boil. Simmer, covered, over low heat until the rice is tender, about 15 minutes. Dry the rice, uncovered, in a moderate oven, 325°F, Gas Mark 3 until the grains are separate and fluffy.
Serves 4

BREADS

Stuffed Parathas

1 lb. (4 cups) wholewheat flour
pinch of salt
water or milk to mix
4 oz. (½ cup) ghee

Filling:
8 oz. (1 cup) potatoes, cooked and
 mashed
1 teaspoon cumin seeds
few coriander leaves, chopped
salt and pepper

Place the flour and salt in a bowl. Mix in enough water or milk to make a firm dough. Divide the dough into 8 portions and roll each into a circle.

Mix the mashed potatoes with the rest of the filling ingredients, adding salt and pepper to taste. Divide the filling evenly between the rounds. Fold each round of dough in half to enclose the filling, then roll into a ball and roll out to a circle, about 6 inches in diameter.

Grease a hot griddle or heavy frying pan (skillet) with a little of the ghee and cook each paratha on both sides until crisp and golden brown. Serve hot.

Serves 8

Pappadoms

Buy pappadoms from an Indian grocer or delicatessen. Fry in hot fat or oil, making sure every part of the pappadom touches the fat, then turn immediately and fry on the other side. Alternatively, brush with melted butter or oil and grill on each side.

Nan Baked Leavened Bread

8 oz. (2 cups) plain (all-purpose)
  flour
½ teaspoon baking powder
½ teaspoon salt
1 teaspoon sugar
1 oz. fresh (1 cake compressed)
  yeast

4 fl. oz. (½ cup) milk
2 oz. (¼ cup) butter or ghee,
  melted
1 tablespoon poppy seeds

In a large mixing bowl sift together the flour, baking powder, salt and sugar. Blend the yeast with 2 tablespoons (3T) of the milk. Warm the remaining milk until lukewarm. Add to the yeast with 1 oz. (2T) of the melted butter or ghee; mix well.

Make a hollow in the centre of the flour and gradually pour in the yeast mixture, stirring it into the flour until the liquid is absorbed. Knead well for about 15 minutes, until the dough is smooth and springy. Add a little more flour if it is sticky.

Cover with a cloth, or put the dough in a lightly oiled polythene (plastic) bag and leave to rise until it has doubled in bulk, about 2 hours at average room temperature.

Divide the dough into 8 portions and roll each one into a ball with floured hands. Cover the dough with a cloth and leave for about 15 minutes.

Flatten each ball into a circle. Brush the tops with melted butter and sprinkle with poppy seeds. Place the rounds of dough on greased baking sheets and bake in a hot oven at 450°F, Gas Mark 8 for about 10 minutes, until the bread is puffed up and brown.
Makes 8

Chappatis

8 oz. (2 cups) wholewheat flour   butter or ghee
pinch of salt
¼ pint (⅔ cup) water (approximately)

Put the flour and salt into a large mixing bowl and make a hollow in the centre. Add the water gradually, working in the flour to make a firm dough. Knead well for about 15 minutes, until the dough is smooth. Cover with a damp cloth and leave to stand for about 30 minutes. The dough should be quite firm and hard.

Divide the dough into 8 portions. Roll each into a circle, about 6 inches in diameter, sprinkling the rolling pin and work surface with flour to prevent sticking.

Fry each chappati in a very hot heavy frying pan, without fat. When the top surface shows signs of bubbling, turn the chappati over and cook for 30-40 seconds on the other side. Then place the chappati under a warm grill (broiler) until it puffs up. Spread butter or ghee on one side, fold over and serve hot.
Makes 8

Puris

4 oz. (1 cup) wholewheat flour   1 oz. (2T) butter, melted
4 oz. (1 cup) plain (all-purpose)   ¼ pint (⅔ cup) water
   flour   (approximately)
½ teaspoon salt   oil for deep frying

Combine the dry ingredients in a large mixing bowl. Make a hollow in the centre and pour in the melted butter. Add the water gradually, kneading the mixture, until a firm dough is formed. Continue to knead for a further 5-10 minutes. Cover with a damp cloth and set aside for 15 minutes.

Divide the dough into 8 pieces and roll each into a thin circle, 4-5 inches in diameter. Fry the puris, one at a time, in the hot oil. After a few seconds the puris will puff up. Press down with a fish slice or the back of a spoon. When the puris are crisp and golden, remove from the oil and drain on kitchen paper. Serve hot.
Makes 8

Variation:
To make cocktail puris, break off small pieces of dough and roll into circles, 1½ inches in diameter. As soon as they are cooked, sprinkle with sesame salt or celery salt.

     CHAPPATIS AND PURIS *(Photograph: McDougalls Country Life Wheatmeal Flour)*

SWEET DISHES

Jelabi

8 oz. (2 cups) plain (all-purpose)
  flour
pinch of salt
½ oz. fresh (½ cake compressed)
  yeast
pinch of saffron, soaked in 1
  tablespoon warm water

3 tablespoons (¼ cup) natural
  (unflavored) yogurt
4 oz. (½ cup) sugar
½ pint (1¼ cups) water
1 teaspoon rose water
oil for deep frying

Sift the flour and salt into a bowl. Dissolve the yeast in 2 teaspoons warm water. Pour the saffron through a fine strainer. Combine the saffron liquid with the yeast and yogurt. Make a hollow in the centre of the flour, pour in the yeast mixture and beat into the flour to give a batter of the consistency of thick cream. If it is too thick, add a little water. Cover the bowl and leave the batter to stand for about 1 hour.

Put the sugar in a pan with the water and dissolve over low heat. When it is dissolved, raise the heat and boil until a thick syrup is formed. Cool the syrup and add the rose water.

Pour the batter into a forcing bag fitted with a ¼ inch plain nozzle. Heat the oil in a deep fryer. Pipe figure-of-eight shapes directly into the hot oil and cook for about 1 minute until they are puffed up and golden brown. Drain the jelabi and immerse in the syrup for 1-2 minutes, then drain and serve.

Serves 4

Barfi

1 ¾ pints (4 ½ cups) milk
2 oz. (¼ cup) sugar
2 oz. (½ cup) pistachio nuts,
  chopped
2 oz. (½ cup) ground almonds

½ teaspoon cardamom seeds,
  crushed
few drops of green colouring
silver paper to decorate (optional)

Pour the milk into a heavy pan, bring to the boil and simmer, uncovered, until it has reduced by half. Add the sugar and dissolve over low heat.

Mix the pistachio nuts, almonds and cardamom seeds and add to the pan. Stir well and continue to cook, stirring, until the mixture is thick. Blend in a few drops of green colouring to give a delicate green colour.

Pour the mixture into a greased shallow dish or tin and decorate with silver paper, if liked. When cool, cut the barfi into squares.
Serves 4

Nan Khatai Coconut Biscuits (Cookies)

9 oz. (2 ¼ cups) plain (all-purpose)
  flour
1 ½ teaspoons baking powder
½ teaspoon ground cardamom
½ teaspoon salt
10 oz. (1 ¼ cups) castor
  (superfine) sugar

8 oz. (1 cup) butter, softened
2 eggs, beaten
granulated sugar
desiccated (shredded) coconut

Sift together the flour, baking powder, cardamom and salt. Beat together the castor sugar and butter until the mixture is pale and fluffy. Gradually beat in the eggs, adding a little flour between each addition. Then fold in the remaining flour.

Drop teaspoonfuls of the dough onto ungreased baking sheets, spacing well apart. Flatten to form small rounds about ⅛ inch thick, using a glass covered with a damp cloth. Sprinkle with granulated sugar and coconut.

Bake in a moderately hot oven at 375°F, Gas Mark 5, for 8-10 minutes, or until the biscuits are lightly browned around the edges. Leave them on the baking sheets for about 30 seconds, then transfer to a wire rack and leave to cool. Store in well sealed tins or jars until required.
Makes about 60

Coconut Squares

2 pints (5 cups) milk
4 oz. (½ cup) sugar
4 oz. (1⅓ cups) fresh, grated, or
  desiccated (shredded) coconut

1 teaspoon rose water
few drops of pink colouring
silver paper to decorate (optional)

Pour the milk into a heavy pan, bring to the boil and let it simmer, uncovered, until reduced by half, stirring frequently. Add the sugar and dissolve over low heat. Then stir in the coconut and continue cooking and stirring until the mixture is very thick. Stir in the rose water.

Turn half the mixture into a greased shallow dish or tin. Add the colouring to the remaining mixture, tinting it a pale pink colour. Then spread on top of the white layer in the tin.

Cool then cut into squares. Decorate with silver paper, if liked.
Serves 4

Banana Halwa

6 large bananas, peeled
3 tablespoons (¼ cup) ghee or
  clarified butter
½ pint (1¼ cups) water

6 oz. (¾ cup) sugar
½ teaspoon ground cardamom
¼ teaspoon rose essence

Cut the bananas into 1 inch pieces. Heat the ghee or clarified butter in a pan over moderate heat and fry the bananas, stirring, for 4-5 minutes until soft. Remove from the heat and mash the bananas with 3 tablespoons (¼ cup) of the water.

Return to the heat and cook for 2-3 minutes, stirring constantly. In a separate pan, dissolve the sugar in the remaining water over low heat. Pour the syrup over the bananas. Continue cooking, stirring frequently, for 15-20 minutes until the mixture is quite thick. Stir in the cardamom and rose essence.

Spread the mixture into a 6 × 4 inch buttered dish. Allow to cool. Cut into small squares and chill before serving.
Serves 8

BEEF AND PINEAPPLE CURRY WITH RICE *(page 62)*
(Photograph: The Rice Council)

Gulab Jamon — Spiced Cream Dessert in Syrup

1 lb. (2 cups) sugar
1¼ pints (3 cups) water
¾ teaspoon rose water
2 tablespoons (3T) flour
8 oz. (2⅔ cups) non-fat dried milk
  powder (dry milk solids)

¼ pint (⅔ cup) double (heavy)
  cream
8 whole cardamoms
2 oz. (⅓ cup) raisins
1 oz. (¼ cup) almonds, chopped
oil for deep frying

Put the sugar and water in a pan over very low heat. When the sugar has dissolved, raise the heat and cook to a thick syrup. Allow the syrup to cool, then add the rose water. Pour the syrup into a glass serving bowl and set aside.

Mix the flour and dried milk in a bowl and gradually add the cream, stirring to form a dough. Crack the cardamoms and separate the seeds.

Take teaspoonfuls of the dough and make a small hollow in the centre of each one. Place a few cardamom seeds, 1-2 raisins and a few chopped almonds in each hollow. Fold the pieces of dough to enclose the filling. Form into 'pillow' shapes.

Deep fry in the hot oil until crisp and golden brown. Drain on kitchen paper. Place in the syrup and serve chilled, allowing 3 per person.
Serves 8

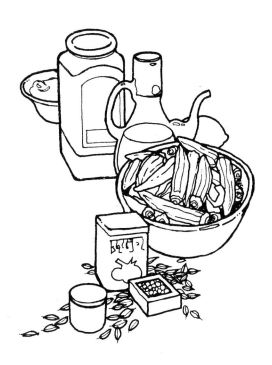

INDEX